Illusion in Plain Sight

Activities Book of Hidden Pictures for Adults

Activibooks

Activibooks
COLORING, DRAWING & ACTIVITY BOOKS
FOR ADULTS

Copyright 2016

FIND the OBJECTS

FIND the OBJECTS

FIND the OBJECTS

FIND the OBJECTS

FIND the OBJECTS

FIND the OBJECTS

FIND the OBJECTS

FIND the OBJECTS

FIND the OBJECTS

FIND the OBJECTS

HELP ME FIND THIS!

FIND the OBJECTS

HELP ME FIND THIS!

HELP ME FIND THIS!

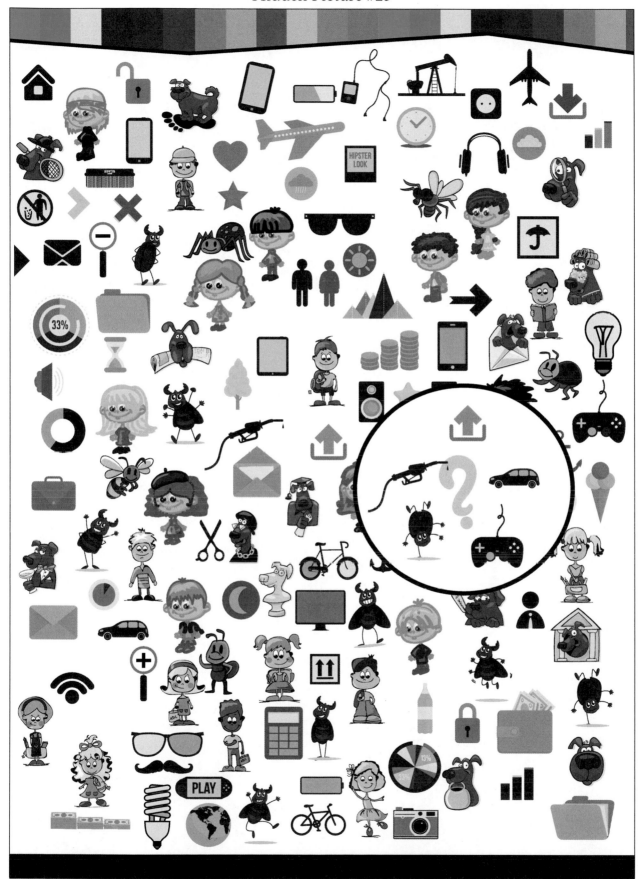

ANSWERS

Answer #1

Answer #2

Answer #3

Answer #4

FIND the OBJECTS

FIND the OBJECTS

FIND the OBJECTS

FIND the OBJECTS

FIND the OBJECTS

FIND the OBJECTS

Answer #15

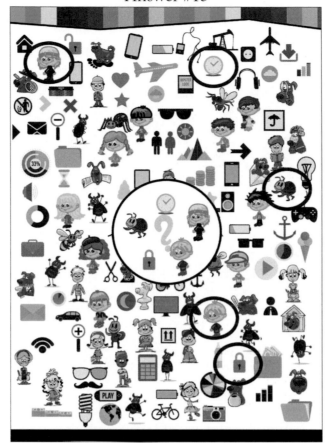

Answer #16

Answer #17

Answer #18

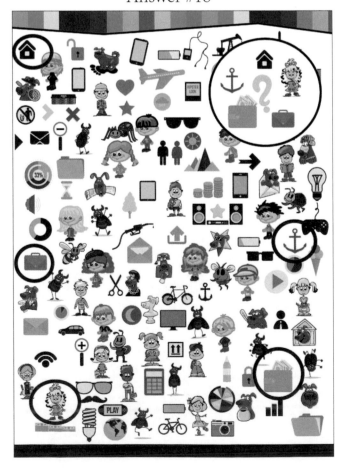

Answer #19

FIND the OBJECTS

Answer #20

Answer #21

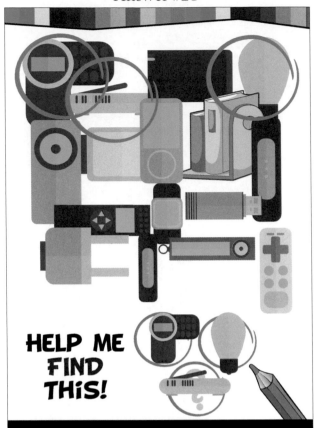

HELP ME FIND THIS!

Answer #22

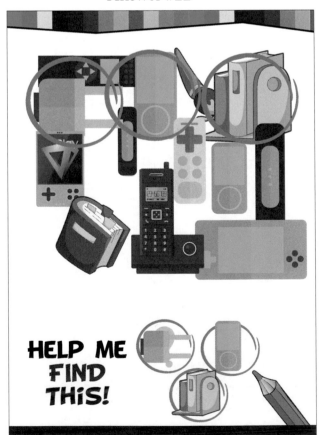

HELP ME FIND THIS!

Answer #23

Answer #24

Made in the USA
San Bernardino, CA
26 May 2020